Touch

Open

Rest

TOUCH OPEN REST

An Encounter of Total Victory

Kenechukwu Amanambu. C

XULON PRESS

Xulon Press
2301 Lucien Way #415
Maitland, FL 32751
407.339.4217
www.xulonpress.com

© 2022 by Kenechukwu Amanambu. C

All rights reserved solely by the author. The author guarantees all contents are original and do not infringe upon the legal rights of any other person or work. No part of this book may be reproduced in any form without the permission of the author.

Due to the changing nature of the Internet, if there are any web addresses, links, or URLs included in this manuscript, these may have been altered and may no longer be accessible. The views and opinions shared in this book belong solely to the author and do not necessarily reflect those of the publisher. The publisher therefore disclaims responsibility for the views or opinions expressed within the work.

Unless otherwise indicated, Scripture quotations taken from the King James Version (KJV) – *public domain*.

Paperback ISBN-13: 978-1-6628-5751-5
Ebook ISBN-13: 978-1-6628-5752-2

Table of Contents

Acknowledgment vii
Preface ix
Introduction xi

Section A: Touch

Chapter 1   Press 1
Chapter 2   Key 12
Chapter 3   The Way 23

Section B: Open

Chapter 4   Newness 35
Chapter 5   The Truth 46

Section C: Rest

Chapter 6   Perfection 55
Chapter 7   Joy 64
Chapter 8   The Life 71

Acknowledgment

I appreciate Minister Nnedinma for her continuous encouragement in words, prayers, and resources. May the good Lord bless her richly. My profound gratitude goes to the personality of the Holy Spirit who has guided me from the conception and writing of this book.

Thank you, Jesus Christ, for this wonderful piece of work.

Preface

We might ask ourselves: must there be a force before an opening occurs that will lead to rest? My answer is "yes." For God is Almighty to fulfill His Word of the deliverance of His people from slavery. He must find expression of His power and invest His jealousy upon that man to be able to fulfill His promises. There must be a finger of His touch upon such a person, so He gave access (open) to the path of the supernatural, to be able to bring rest to the people, community, and nations. Remember, God's ways are pathfinding.

"Great is the LORD, and greatly to be praised;
And his greatness is unsearchable" (Ps. 145:3).

And Moses said, "I will now then aside and see this great sight, why the bush is not burnt" (Gen. 3:3). It brought amazement to his heart and the Lord saw his heart posture.

Touch, Open, Rest

An encounter happened instantly. The encounter comes in the place of touching with the Divinity (God) before an opening can occur. The state of being open must take an effect before rest will take place.

Let me give you a scenario. When you get back from a hard day of work, having become fatigued, three things happen at the door. First, you unlock your door; that brings touch. Second, you open the door with your hand; bringing you to access. Lastly, you close the door behind you; it brings the day's work to an end in your mind. It brings something else as well which is rest (freedom). That's what our lives are all about when we find our place in Christ Jesus.

Introduction

After the pre-adamic era, God created man in His image and likeness; God destined the uniqueness of man and his purpose of existence.

> *"God said, let us make man in our image, after our likeness: and let them have dominion over the fish of the sea, and over the fowl of the air, and over the cattle, and over all the earth, and over every creeping thing that creepeth upon the earth"* (Gen. 1:26).

This gives him dominion and access to authority to command things and subdue anything beneath man. But man lost his uniqueness in God. His legitimation and power were taken from him due to a lack of knowledge of the forbidden fruit. "My people perish for lack of knowledge" (Hosea 4:6).

Man was eager to have access to what he knew not about, not minding breaking an oath sworn to his Creator (disobedience). For in the day that thou eateth of the tree, thou shall surely die (Gen. 2:17). "In Adam, all died" (Gen. 15:22).

On that very day, man lost all that was rightfully his. His legitimate rule became illegitimate.

Something happened; Jesus came as the second Adam to redeem us to the Father and gave us access to the heavenly throne. Through Him, we have access by one Spirit unto the Father.

> *"For through him we both have access by one Spirit unto the Father"* (Eph. 2:18).

Jesus Christ became the only and rightful living host that links us through touch and that door opens, which results in a rest that we need in God.

> *"Jesus saith unto him, I am the way, the truth, and the life: no man cometh unto the Father, but by me"* (John 14:6).

Introduction

This book will guide you to your place in Christ Jesus. As you read this book, please open your mind and self unto Jesus Christ to take root in your heart. Only He brings rest upon a life. Call unto Him and He will answer thee.

> *"Call unto me, and I will answer thee, and show thee great and mighty things, which thou knowest not"* (Jer. 33:3).

Shalom–Peace!

Section A

TOUCH

Chapter 1

Press

"Then were there brought unto him little children, that he should put his hands on them, and pray; and the disciples rebuked them" (Matt. 19:13).

Touch is a significant way to have access to whatever you want. For instance, to climb up the mountain, you must have access to a rope or instrument that will help you get to the top of the mountain and remain steady. While climbing, your hands must press very hard on the rope and your legs steadfast on the mountain.

In the above Scripture, the parents knew that Jesus Christ had something so powerful and unique that they, as stewards, didn't have. They were not able to give because they, as the parents, needed what Jesus had. The decision was made within them that if they didn't have and couldn't get, let the children have such that is within this man; touch can be a connection to something. The children's parents were scolded for bothering the Lord Jesus. Not realizing they were stopping a blessing of change upon the lives of the children. In their hearts, they were protecting the Master but preventing the little ones from accessing their greater glory.

> *"And now, brethren, I wot that through ignorance ye did it, as did also your rulers"* (Acts 3:17).

Matthew 19:15 says, *"And he laid his hands on them and departed thence."* He touched him by pressing something into their spirit.

When we touch the Lord, something is pressed into our lives; a change occurs like the woman with the issue of blood. Mark 5:25-34

That will bring us back to the chapter titled; PRESS.

What is "press?" The Oxford Dictionary explains that press is a move or cause to move into a position of contact with something by exerting continuous physical force.

The intellectual explanation means moving something in a particular direction when you keep exerting force on it. But that's not the case for God. When you press on Him, He puts His hands on you, He repairs you, extends your life, saves you from destruction and sows His jealousy and presence upon you. Come unto me, all ye that labor and are heavy laden, and I will give you rest.

Let's explain "press" deeper using my own defined acronym:

P–Put
R–Repair
E–Extend
S–Save
S–Sow

PUT

In the Scripture, it was stated in the beginning of Matthew 19:13 that He should put His hands on them. The other word for "put" is "lay." When Jesus put His hands on them, He was pulling unclean traits from the lives of the little ones. He knew that was the first thing that needed to be done before impacting something into them. In that particular verse, "put" came before pray. You can't sow on untilled land; you first have to till the land and cultivate your crops.

For you to earmark your place in Christ, you must allow Him to pull unclean traits from your lives which can be stubbornness, pride in life, or ruthlessness against people. Jesus just needs your simple faith as the little children did to believe in Him.

> *"For we walk by faith, not by sight"* (2 Cor. 5:7).

The little children believed so much with joy and He was willing to put His hand on them. Their faith attracted a touch of change upon them.

> *"Joshua the son of Nun called the priests, and said unto them, 'Take up the ark of the covenant, and let seven priests bear seven trumpets of ram's horns before the ark of the LORD'"* (Josh. 6:6).

Joshua was instructing the priests on the directions of the Lord for them to take up (to press tightly) upon the ark of God on their shoulders. The "take-up" means to press firmly; to touch and never lose your grip upon it. The Lord knew the battle was more than the physical eyes could see or bear. He instructed the priests to lead the way with the ark so he could put an end to the spiritual wall (barrier) standing against God's people entering into their promised land. In other words, He needed to bring out the best from His people by inserting His sovereignty on the wall.

When we allow His hands to be put upon us, we become valuable earthen vessels for the Lord.

> *"That David behaved himself more wisely than all the servants of Saul; so that his name was much set by"* (1 Sam. 18:30b).

REPAIR

> *"Some of you will rebuild the deserted ruins of your cities. Then you will be known as a*

rebuilder of walls and a restorer of homes" (Isa. 58:12).

When you receive a touch of God, He repairs your spiritual artilleries, emotional damage is reset back to the right form, and your physically damaged tissues are repaired. You function properly the way our Creator has made you to be. God's touch fixes every loophole your past has created. If the foundations are destroyed, what can the righteous do? Nothing, except you meet the original manufacturer.

For instance, when you contract a mining project to the Chinese; have in mind that everything will be written in Chinese if they omit translating it to English. It will be a problem for Americans when such a project need repairing.

The good news is that our God (the Creator of the universe) can repair, rebuild, and restore anything in our lives and environment when we cry unto His touch. No matter the mountain we face in life, it is like a cross over in the eyes of God. Abraham has a mountain (childless) until he found something (touch). The touch of God made him know and have the experiential knowledge of God. That was when the door of true fatherhood opened unto him (Isaac). Laughter smiled at him. Our infallible proof as Christians is when we constantly touch the Lord. Abraham's constant touch through obedience, hospitality, and kindness came about the promise.

EXTEND

> *"Surely goodness and Mercy shall follow me all the days of my life and I will dwell in the house of the LORD forever"* (Ps. 23:6).

His goodness speaks about the grace He bestows on us. The touch of Jesus brings an extension of grace (goodness) to those that seek Him. Then He extends His touch, life, and His presence (nearness) to that person or people. If I extend my hands toward you, that means I am reaching out to you; either to give you something, to save you, or a hand of friendship.

> *"For God so loved the world that he gave his only begotten son, that whosoever believeth in him should not perish, but have everlasting life"* (John 3:16).

God gave (extended) His hand of love to mankind by extending His everlasting life to us through Jesus Christ, so we can live. His giving brought about reconciliation between Him (God) and man. Something must go that's worthy of an extension through His everlasting bridge of access.

Through the extension of His touch, He showered His kindness on us, along with all wisdom and understanding.

God is extending His hand of touch toward you, reach out to Him and receive those supernatural riches in kindness and grace.

SAVE

> *"For the wages of sin is death; but the gift of God is eternal life through Jesus Christ our Lord"* (Rom. 6:23).

The touch of Jesus brought about salvation upon mankind. It is done and settled. There is no form of application or form that you need to sign or rituals that need to be performed to be saved. His death upon the cross was the greatest gift given to mankind because something unique was shed on that cross; the precious blood of the Lamb. The uniqueness of the gift made it so magnificent unto any man that runs to Him for freedom.

> *"Who hath delivered us from the power of darkness, and hath translated us into the kingdom of His dear Son?"* (Col. 1:13).

If there was no death, there wouldn't be gifting. If there was no gifting, there wouldn't be a transference side of external life (Kingdom of His dear Son and having authority with an understanding of Him). His touch resisted and saved us from the notch of enemies in our lives. The devil, since the inception of the fall of man, has tormented man with the punishment of death. But the Savior, Jesus, came and gave us life in abundance. He saved us and restored us to our position.

SOW

> *"And the seed whose fruit is righteousness is sown in peace by those who make peace"* (James 3:18).

Jesus's touch brings peace. He is the Prince of Peace. When you come to Him, you must regain your peace; no matter the situation of life you are passing through.

> *"For I am persuaded, that neither death, nor life, nor angels, nor principalities, nor powers, nor things present nor things to come. Nor height, nor depth nor any other creature, shall be able to separate us from the love of God, which is in Christ Jesus our Lord"* (Rom. 8:38-39).

His love signifies peace eternal; not the peace the world sows into our lives. The mundane things are temporary. The peace that's been sown in our lives is the fountain of life. It can never run dry, even amid problems. Righteousness, peace, and joy in the Holy Ghost are infused in our lives when we touch. His torch brings about a sowing, a divine revelation of Him, an embodiment of His grace and truth.

Christ is the great sower in our lives.

And He said, *"The one who sows the good seed is the Son of Man"* (Matt. 13:37).

Remember, you need to surrender everything at His feet to be able to access that which He has sown. He said, "It is finished" (John 19:30). Victory had been sown, blessings had been sown, authority had been sown, God's Kingship had been sown, and His dominion had been sown. Just reach out to the sower and get yours.

I see you flying higher with wings of an eagle of power and might.

Chapter 2

Key

> *"And the key of the house of David will I lay upon his shoulders, so he shall open, and none shall shut; and he shall shut, and none shall open"* (Isa. 22:22).

The house of David signifies a chamber of royalty; a place kings, queens, princes, and princess's dwell; divine beings that can't be seen in any place but the Kingdom. The best of things is found in a royal home. A key is now given to someone unique for our sake, making him take the highest position in the royal court; not just putting out his hand, but to be laid on his shoulders.

When a heavy-weight boxer is coming to a match, he either carries the belt on his shoulder or wears it on his waist.

The shoulder signifies a champion. That champion which I speak of is Jesus Christ, the universal King. While the belt on His waist signifies that He is still reigning, He is in charge of this tournament. The key has been given to us, the children of God through the ultimate sacrifice of Jesus Christ on the cross. He died and took the key from the devil.

> *"I am he that liveth, and was dead; and, behold, I am alive for evermore, amen; and have the Keys of hell and of death"* (Rev. 1:18).

If Christ Jesus had not yet succeeded, He wouldn't have given Peter the keys of the Kingdom which is full of mysteries and powers.

> *"And I will give unto thee the keys of the kingdom of heaven; and whatsoever thou shalt bind on earth shall be bound in heaven and whatsoever thou shalt loose on earth shall be loosed in heaven"* (Matt. 16:19).

That was a free license for an encounter given to Peter from the Lord. Do you know we are also a partaker of such encounters? You and I are not excluded from the equation. Remember when He died, He rose, we went with Him to that upper echelon, and He gave a gift to all men.

I want to sincerely ask you a question. If you are giving someone a key, does your hand touch the person receiving it? If your answer is 'yes,' that means the touch of God comes with power and glory. It is given to us. The word *key* in the Kingdom of God stands for something extraordinary. I want to pour out my heart on what the Holy Spirit has revealed concerning the word *key*.

KNOWLEDGE

Knowledge means having an in-depth understanding of the will, purpose, and mind of God, information or of being learned; an instance can be in information or wisdom.

> *"The fear of the LORD is the beginning of Knowledge: but fools despise wisdom and instruction"* (Prov. 1:7).

For you to obtain the knowledge of God, there must be reverence (respect). The word *reverence* shouldn't result in you shaking as if you are meeting or speaking to something or someone that will harm you. No, it means honor with absolute respect as your manufacturer (Creator), your God. When you give to Him, He pours out His knowledge unto you (Prov. 2:6b). Remember, our God is love.

The knowledge I am talking about is not the earthly knowledge but the one that comes from above; that only He can give to those who reverence (respect) Him. That knowledge supersedes the great scientists of this world.

I am talking about when you're able to fully perceive, notice, attentively recognize, or discern without your imagination or reasoning. This knowledge is called epiginosko in Greek, which means the advantage of knowing the purpose of God.

"By his knowledge the depths are broken up, and the clouds drop down the dews" (Prov. 3:20).

Let's take a look at the line; His knowledge of the depths is broken. What that line means is that in the knowledge of God, deep fountains of the earth burst forth. Things in our lives that look very difficult are burst open, it becomes very easy to encompass. Power is released to you through His touch.

The **open** means to **know**.

The **burst** means to **ledge**.

To **know** is to be aware of through observation or inquiry.

Ledge is a narrow, horizontal surface projecting from a wall, cliff, or another surface; having prominence or a step ahead that brings us complete word knowledge. This kind of knowledge does not come except when the Lord's Spirit dwells in the life of a man.

> *"For this cause we also, since the day we heard it, do not cease to pray for you, and to desire that ye might be filled with the knowledge of His will in all wisdom and spiritual understanding"* (Col. 1:9).

Kindly seek the knowledge of God that heightens so many things on Earth.

EMPOWERS

Empowers signifies being given full access of authority over something. When God empowers you, you begin to flow in His presence.

> *"Then he called his twelve disciples together, and gave them power and authority over all devils, and to cure diseases"* (Luke 9:1).

In 2018, it seemed as if every door had been shut on me. Nothing was happening. It is not that I did not know God, but the power of darkness over my life and destiny was so overwhelming that I cried unto the Lord and He instructed me to go into prayer and fasting for forty days. During that period of fasting, a spirit came into my room and breathed an air of fire upon me and told me to receive power. When I woke up, I felt like a new me. I kept on praying that the doors would suddenly open. But after the prayers, days went by, weeks went by, and it got into months; then things began to change for me. Doors began to open in my life. I began to see the light at the end of the tunnel as He empowered me for dominion.

That's what happened to His disciples as the impossible became possible. Things gave way on their own accord, without struggle. They were living in the world of sight and sound but they were not slaves to the stimuli that surrounded them. Because the presence of God had rested upon them when he touched the twelve, they began to rule over circumstances, no matter what was happening.

When He empowers you, your mentality changes; you will start operating or responding calmly and confidently, remembering that He is with you.

His empowerment resonates His presence. In His presence, there is fullness of joy, perfect peace, and unfailing love. It eradicates all darkness from your life and gives abundant light upon a person, people, or church.

> *"And if the spirit of him that raised up Jesus from the dead dwell in you, he that raised up Christ from the dead shall also quicken your mortal bodies by his spirit that dwelleth in you"* (Rom. 8:11).

That empowerment comes from the personality of the Holy Spirit. The Holy Spirit enables and teaches us the gateway of eternal life for those who believe in Jesus Christ. The Spirit resides within us now by faith and by faith we are certain to live with Christ forever. Most of us are ready to know the Holy Spirit. If you refuse Him, empowerment is denied entry into your life. You must be thirsty for Him as the deer pants for streams of water, so your soul must pant for the Holy Spirit.

> *"That I may know him, the power of his resurrection, and the fellowship of his suffering being made conformable unto his death"* (Phil. 3:10).

Make Him your partner and best friend. You will begin to enjoy the free flow of His divine presence.

Let me paraphrase this Bible verse for better understanding:

> *"His empowerment comes unto our lives when our heart's been knitted with the heart of God."*
> Proverbs 23:26

You can't reign on this earth effectively if you're not empowered. Seek His touch and He will empower you.

YOU

> *"Thou shalt also decree a thing, and it shall be established unto thee and the light shall shine upon thy ways"* (Job 22:28).

In this place of the Bible, you read on the word *thou*; it means *you*. God emphatically speaks to us from the beginning of the Scripture to the end; from Genesis to Revelation, God has been talking to you and me.

In this particular verse, the power to become is already deposited in us. And Jesus Christ said, *"but when the Comforter is come"* (John 15:26); meaning the comforter who is the Holy Spirit. A brand-new engine like no other that can't be manufactured by any man. It's already been given to us. That's the spirit of truth. It lives within you to empower you for a greater dimension. When you now decree a thing as the Spirit comes alive, whatever you say speaks volumes. A brand-new engine can't be the same as a used engine; the sound and the life span differs; the engines can't be compared.

> *"So shall my word be that goeth forth out of my mouth: it shall not return unto me void, but it shall accomplish that which I please, and it shall prosper in the thing where to I sent it"* (Isa. 55:11).

You become a true representative of Christ, because now you're a witness of Him. His Spirit beareth witness with your spirit (Rom. 2:16). The rivers of water within you begin to flow like a current in the oceans, in more exceedingly measures.

When God brings His hand down toward you, He touches you. So, He can lift you to become a lamp to the life of men.

If there is no touch of God, there won't be a rush (speed) in your destiny. You receive by the spirit of the Lord or the touch of the devil, make up your mind today, and allow the

King of Glory to illuminate you with His hand of power. Do you not desire a change; a new stature, both physical and spiritual? I do want a change and I am always ready to touch Him daily.

I see the power of God touching you and your household. Whatever is dark in your life, see His Spirit moving over your life in the name of Jesus Christ. Amen.

Your wait doesn't lead you to waste, but it gives you a taste. If you endure to the end, you will have a tasteful life and emerge victorious.

Chapter 3

The Way

"Jesus saith unto him, 'I am the way...'"
(John 14:6).

Why must He say that, "He is the way?" Are there no other ways?

For the wages of sin is death but the gift of God is eternal life through Christ Jesus, our Lord.

To give you an idea of what am saying; let's input ways in the place of wages. "For the wages (ways) of sin is death." That means two ways are given to man; the light and darkness. The choice is yours. We are only creatures given the will to decide what we want. Part B of the Scripture states another way, which is in Christ Jesus,

"But the free gift of God is eternal life" (Rom. 6:23).

The way signifies a gift, another system through Christ Jesus. Eternal life is a gift from God. A gift is not something that we can earn or something that must be paid back. Consider the foolishness of someone who receives a gift given out of love and then offers to pay for it. A gift cannot be purchased by the recipient. He made Himself a way so that we can be saved because of His mercy and not for any good thing we have done (Titus 3:5). There is always a need to be thankful at all times for the gift of God; the way of Christ Jesus that has been bestowed upon us through His sacrifice.

"For through him we both have access by one Spirit unto the Father" (Eph. 2:18).

The Most High God is offering a better path of redemption, route, and link to be free from oppression into a dimension of greatness to reign as kings that we have been created to be. Jesus is nearby with His strong arms extended toward you, offering help to you.

The Way

> *"By a new and living way, which he hath Consecrated for us, through the veil, that is to say, his flesh"* (Heb. 10:20).

The living way is a life-giving way into the most Holy place. For instance, when you go into an office building or an industrial building, there are specifications or directions on ways to follow; which door is needed to pass through, the one that is prohibited for entry, and so on. That is what our Lord is telling us; those other ways over prohibited and restricted ways to destruction.

He gave us a brighter way because He is Yahweh.

That way has been touched by sacrificial blood. It might be narrow but it is safer than the broader way. The sprinkling blood has created a fortified will in that way. Those that follow the narrow path can't be harmed. He will give His angels charge over thee so that you won't dash your feet against a stone. If they eventually come toward that way to attack you, they will flee, because you dwell in the secret place of the Most High God that contains His shadow. Shadow means 'roofing'. When you roof a house properly, there is no way rain can come into the building. His blood is a shadow in that way.

If you keep His ways while following Him, He will lead and protect you.

> "*For I have kept the ways of the LORD, and have not wickedly departed from my God*" (Ps. 15:21).

I love that man of Galilee; He has done so much for you and me despite our failure and faults. He was not selfish or self-centered till death. He never wanted to be the only Son of God. He died and made a way for others to become sons and to have access to the Father. Glory!

> "*Having predestined us unto the adoption of children by Jesus Christ to himself, according to the good pleasure of his will*" (Eph. 1:5).

There is a hymn called "All the Way to Calvary" by the Brooklyn Tabernacle Choir that always reminds me of the way He took and made Himself access to the way. He became the Way for us all.

All the *way* to Calvary
He *went* for me
Jesus *went* for me
He *went* for me
He *died* to set me *free*

Let me explain the significance of the words that are in italics:

Went–A pardon walk for the saint and the unsaved.
Way–Pathway to a place.
Died–The old must be buried for the new to come into effect; restoration of man unto glory.
Free–Authority with liberty to all who come that way.

There are so many benefits and blessings in that way. He wants us to enjoy all that He possesses. He wanted us to partake of His divine nature. He wants us to be king as He is.

> *"And what is the exceeding greatness of his power to us-ward who believe, according to the working of his mighty power"* (Eph. 1:19).

Your belief gives you access to the way.

It is not a tranquil way, but the greatest way given to man. You can't walk in that way with your human dimensions or flesh. The supernatural being leading that way won't give you a helping hand. You need to surrender all to Him. Let Him lead you (Ps. 5:8). Two major forces guide or strengthen the saved and the saints on that part of the journey.

> *"Have mercy upon me, O God, according to thy loving-kindness: according unto the multitude of thy tender mercies blot out my transgressions"* (Ps. 51:1).

Mercy and love are the two major factors that strengthen us in that way.

Mercy

Mercy knows no greater pleasure than to give aid to those without hope. Mercy can't be over-emphasized on this issue.

> *"But when he saw the multitude, he was moved with compassion on them, because they fainted, and were scattered abroad as sheep having no shepherd"* (Matt. 9:36).

His compassionate heart illustrated how merciful our Lord can be. How about those who choose to walk in the way? He will surely ask His angels to encamp all around those who made Him their way.

Mercy is durable riches; you can't get that from the stock market or cryptocurrency or your father's inheritance. It's for those who had prepared their heart for the way, no matter the way circumstances of life have treated you. His mercy can't make you ashamed, instead, He lights you up through His path you follow.

> *"As he journeyed, he came new Damascus and suddenly a light shone around him from heaven"* (Acts 9:4).

You can't be on that way after He has touched you and the enemy comes to seize you. He will blindfold them all for your sake.

His touch brings a launch into a greater atmosphere.

Jesus was merciful till death while on Earth. As He prayed for His offenders in this manner; "Father, forgive them for they know not what they do." It was a cry of an in-depth passion for His care toward us. Now, He has imputed that mercy upon us when we lead people to Christ in our place of work. There is a need to show mercy, which is kindness to people around you irrespective of whom they are or their religion.

> *And the master of the servant was moved with compassion, and loosed him and forgave him the debt"* (Matt. 18:27).

The mercy of God loses us from any yoke.

As I speak into your life right now, receive the mercy of God. The mercies of David will locate you, no matter what you are passing through, in Jesus's name.

Love

"For God so loved the world that he gave his only begotten son…" (John 3:16).

Love is the totality of God's creation. God is love. He demonstrated it by giving us His beloved Son. Who is man that God is so mindful of? God went to such an extent to sacrifice what He cherished. I now understand in Ephesians 1:4 that He chose us in Him before the foundation of the world so that we can live without blame before Him in love.

"Though I speak with the tongues of men and of angels, but have not love, I have become sounding brass or a clanging cymbal" (1 Cor. 13:1).

Sounding brass explains being deceitful. Tares can't be among the wheat. Separation must occur to remove the bad eggs. You must be spotless in your love. If God touches you, these two factors become effectual in your life. A true witness of His mercy and love will be seen in you. You will also witness

His presence in your daily life. For those who witness Christ to others, these three factors come without difficulties. And they are wisdom, status (power), and favor (Luke 2:52).

These are the five beatitudes of Christ's grace; when He touches as you decide to follow the way.

He promised He would never leave nor forsake us when we come to the way; the place of encounter, a place of change, and a place of joy and everlasting peace.

> *"The way of the Lord is strength to the upright: but destruction shall be to the workers of iniquity"* (Prov. 10: 29).

Section B

OPEN

Chapter 4

Newness

> *"God remembered Rachel and God listened to her, and opened her womb"* (Gen. 30:22).

Eventually, God answered Rachel's prayers and gave her a child of her own. Before God answered her, she had given her servant to Jacob as a concubine. Trusting God when nothing seems to happen is difficult. But it is harder still to live with the consequences of taking matters into our own hands.

When the Lord opens His door upon an individual, it results in newness and fresh air blown on that individual. If you go to visit someone, the door cannot open by itself for you when you walk up to it. Someone needs to come to the door and open it. There is a process before the door opens. You have to knock or ring the bell to notify the owner of the house. If the owner is not attentive to the knocking or sound of the bell, you may remain there for a long time.

In the Scripture written above, God remembered her plight.

> *"He that remembered his covenant forever the word which he commanded to a thousand generations"* (Ps. 105:8).

He remembered who He was: God of fruitfulness, God of mercy, and God of love. He remembered His promises that, *"He makes the barren woman abide in the house as a joyful mother of children. Praise the Lord!"* (Ps. 113:9).

God Remembers

It was the Lord that shut her womb, because of someone's (Leah) agony and rejection. He is not partial (Gen. 29:31). God did not forget about her entirely. Keep in mind that He is God; He decides what He wants. Her book of remembrance was close, as it was in the days of Mordecai. But her time came to wear the garment of newness which represented motherhood for her. Nothing could stop it. Say loudly, *"My time has come!"* Newness brings joy. The book was opened and God remembered her good deed and track record toward Jacob when Rachel met Jacob for the first time (Gen. 29:11-12). The Bible recorded that she ran back home to her father, Jacob, to share the good news and explained things to him. She didn't look down on him nor despise him. But she was full of joy and happiness to be of help not realizing what she was doing and for whom. Do you know most of us have either in one way or another driven out our angel of blessings ignorantly because of our rudeness or unruly behaviors by how we treat or speak (insult) to people?

> *"Be not forgetful to entertain strangers: for thereby some have entertained angels unawares"* (Heb. 13:2).

Her hospitality brought about newness into her life.

God Listens

"And this is the confidence that we have toward him that if we ask anything according to his will, he hears us" (1 John 5:14).

He listens speedily to our prayer when it aligns with His will. And God listened to her. His ears became fully opened because He planned to make her fruitful and replenish the earth. Her seed was needed to fulfill the purpose and plan of God's Kingdom. That is why when we pray, we should do or ask what is in line or will with heaven. When we talk to God, we shouldn't demand what we want; rather, we should ask Him what He wants for us.

When God hears our prayer, it means we are praying with confidence to His will. Our strength in prayer signifies the confidence that He listens.

You need to come to His court with a striking boldness to obtain mercy. You can't prevail in mercy if your boldness is not His will. Let His will become your will-power.

In 2019, I asked God for a car. I prayed for a car; nothing came forth. Was His will associated with my need for a car?

No, I don't think I was considering that. I wanted a car because people were buying cars. I asked God why? He educated me that His will was not in that car. I changed my prayer point to, *"God give me a car for the need of your Kingdom and my personal work in life."* It came speedily; I didn't use my money to purchase the car because I sincerely prayed concerning His will on the car. You must be conscious of your prayer request.

God can do things through us, around us, and within us, because His power (will) lives in us. You have been saying that nothing is working. Turn to His will. You have prayed and yet you have no results. Pray His will. You have been a minister of God and nothing is working. Begin to minister His will. You have been in business, yet nothing is working. Start the business in His will and let the purpose of God's Kingdom find expression in your business venture. He wants you to seek Him first in all you do (Matt. 6:33).

In the life of Rachel, scarcity was in place for newness. A slow burn settled into her life, filled with confusion.

If there is no opposition, there won't be a vacancy for your position.

Our Lord Jesus was prepared for any outcome on the cross at Golgotha. His readiness brought about newness into His name, a name of authority, a name with access. He became King of kings. Just at the mention of that name, things will begin to happen and take shape, both in the physical and spiritual realm such as in Philippians 2:4-11:

The man at the beautiful gate had been lame for forty years begging alms from people entering the temple. The gate's name is called beautiful, but there was no reflection of such beauty in his life having sat at the gate for years. Why was his life ugly, when the gate was beautiful, as it is referred to? Where was his family? Why must they desert him and disgrace him in front of the people? That's the question I kept asking myself. And I realized that men can't give you newness but only God. And then something amazing happened on that fateful day in his fortieth year. God wanted to introduce newness into his life. He sent Peter and John, who were going to the temple. Their coming was orchestrated by God Himself, not Peter nor John. Forty years means new order, transformation, and triumph in Bible numerology. When the apostles spoke into His life, the author of life brought newness to his being. A change occurred; strength came into his bones (Acts 3:7). God is not interested in giving you earthly possessions. His love resonates with a deep passion to give us His life (newness of Him).

> *"If any man be in Christ, he is a new creature: old things are passed away; behold all things are become new"* (2 Cor. 5:17).

Christ Jesus was introduced into His life right there on the spot. Peter said, *"Silver and gold have I none; but such as I have give I thee"* (Acts 3:6). He became a new creature. The old form disappeared; the beggar, as he was known. The fundamental identity of his being ended when newness possessed him, a new scent, a new garment of beauty was worn upon him and the ashes of pain ended. Newness called flourishing came in. He started flourishing in wholeness as a man.

> *"The righteous shall flourish like the palm tree; he shall grow like a cedar in Lebanon"* (Ps. 92:12).

Palm trees are known for their long-life span. To flourish like palm trees means to stand tall and to live long. The palms of the region where this psalm was written are also an excellent source of food, producing dates. Palm trees can't live that long if there is no constant source of nutrients supplied to them. Those who place their faith firmly in God can have the strength and vitality they desire. You become like a tree planted by the rivers of water. Do you know you are an inspiration and expression of God?

The lame man's life was dwindling from the people. When the prince of life came into him, he began to flourish (newness of existence). He knew something transforming had transpired inside and outside of him. His life span was extended. The vitality of life started springing forth. The joy of the Lord rested upon him. He was an expression to behold; he was the talk of the church, city, and nation because newness came into him. You must initiate change to be changed. Have a change in mentality; a definite order of newness. No matter what you are passing through, if you refuse to renew your mind, you can never experience newness in your life and be renewed in the spirit of your mind (Eph. 4:23). You have to keep the thought of your mind in oneness with the spirit of God, to be able to get the best treasure of your life while in existence, deep calls unto deep. New wine can't be poured into an old wine bottle. If you present it to a person or people, they will never accept it as new wine. You can't be ready for change when you can't let go of your past. The past needs to be pulled down and you must come out of it.

> *"For the weapons of our warfare are not carnal, but mighty through God to the pulling down of stronghold; casting down imaginations, and every high thing that exalted itself against the knowledge of God, and bringing into captivity every thought to the obedience of Christ "*(2 Cor. 10:4-5).

Hades, with all its resources and weapons, has succeeded most times in bringing about gloominess in the lives of believers at large. But this particular verse, especially verse 5; casts down imaginations; meaning everything that stands in your way to possess in the newness must be cast down. And it must start with your imagination (thought). If you keep thinking of failure and you are praying to God for newness in your job or to have a better life, it will never come to pass. Your thought should align with your confession.

It wasn't until Rachel forgot her pain and became joyful with her sister and her children, celebrating their happiness with them even when she was barren, that God then remembered her. Her womb opened. Newness brings about reformation in a person. When I mention reformation, I speak about the character of the individual. God can't use a person whose character doesn't conform to the likeness of our maker. This is something to which we need to pay close attention. It speaks of the formation of our nature and the cultivation of our habits. It is more than merely having an experience before God; it involves the formation of character.

You must develop the ability to sit down, listen, and discover the real issue which you have heard. *"He fastened his eyes on them, by giving head unto them, expecting to receive something of them"* (Acts 3:5). You must consistently be in expectation for newness. Sorrow may endure for a night, but I assure you that joy will surely come in the morning. Sorrow can't last forever. What is constant in life is change. We must change into His newness.

Hope defiled destroys readiness of newness.

Let's keep our hearts and thoughts open in expectation of the newness of things.

I prophesy into your life that any power that won't allow you to step into your ordained newness by God; let that power be destroyed right now in the name of Jesus Christ, the Son of the living God.

> *"He disappointed the devices of the crafty so that their hands cannot perform their enterprise"* (Job 5:12).

Chapter 5

The Truth

"For God so loved the world that he gave his only begotten son, that whosoever believeth in him, shall have everlasting Life" (John 3:16).

Let's put the word (truth) in the above Bible verse,

For God so loved the world, that He gave the truth, that whosoever believes in the truth, shall have everlasting life.

The 'word 'love' was the grace opened to the truth, while the giving established the truth. For you to access or to know the truth, you have to first obtain grace (love). If you don't have love for what you believe or who you believe, you will not know the truth about the person or system (organization). You have to love what you are trusting. Total trust is needed to know the depth of that thing. The truth encompasses an extensive truth. *"And ye shall know the truth, and the truth will set you free"* (John 8:32). If you don't believe in the truth, you will lack access to the all-knowing.

> *"But ye have the unction from the Holy one, and ye know all the things"* (1 John 2:20).

Then you will know the truth. Your foreseen knowledge about Jesus Christ (Son of the living God), who is the truth, brings about liberation. In Proverbs 24:5, it tells us that knowledge is power. That's true. Your ability to know and understand makes you top-notch over every existing being or spiritual force, wherever you find yourself. If you desire to make known the truth (Jesus Christ), the truth opens up to you; things that you can't comprehend with your human perception or reasoning. Don't say or desire not to have the truth. The truth is a light to our path. The truth is a lamp unto thy feet. A great key opens one to access the light offered to man.

Many believers or churches are not really of the opinion that the truth is worth knowing. Ignorance sets in because they lack knowledge and that has caused so many believers to perish. When you reject knowing Jesus, you have rejected God the Father and also the all-knowing, whereby the Holy Spirit can never find expression in your life. The Holy Spirit is the Spirit of truth but not the truth. He is the medium for us to have access to the truth. Only the truth who is Jesus Christ our Lord can glorify the Father. We are witnesses to the truth. We can't access the father except when we honor and believe the son (the truth).

Our inability to comprehend the truth has caused disabilities in our life.

> *"It is the Spirit that quickeneth; the flesh profiteth nothing: the words that I speak unto you, they are spirit, and they are life"* (John 6:63).

I want you to leave your heart unlatched. Light is about to bolt in with speed, as I unravel the mystery from the Scripture unto you. I am going to insert the word, the truth, and open into a Scripture;

> *"And whatsoever ye shall ask in the truth,"* that will open, *that the Father may glorified in the*

truth. If ye shall ask anything in the truth, I will open" (John 14:13-14).

In that particular verse of the Bible, I inserted the truth where my name should be. Remember, the name of Jesus is the only source of a real truth that we seek or need. Please kindly accept the changes for your understanding on what I'm trying to portray.

Without the truth, there won't be an opening to the route of light.

Your adequacy to the truth breaks you out of the darkness. If Hannah had never known much about God of Shiloh, she would still be barren and the prophet Samuel wouldn't have proceeded from her. Her knowledge gave her a breaking forth into motherhood.

Immediately after my graduation in 2008, I was ready for my NYSC (National Youth Service Corps). It is a program set up by the Nigerian government to involve Nigerian graduates in nation-building and the development of the country. I was expecting to be among batch A for the program, but my name was not on the list of those who were shortlisted. I became perturbed and depressed, asking myself what was wrong. I went into prayer, utilizing the truth (Jesus Christ) to know what was wrong in the realm of the Spirit. God revealed to me that a person was sitting on my result. It was sent to the governing council to enlist my name that was to be sent for the program. I commanded that that person in my dream should get off from my result in the name of Jesus (the truth) and immediately light sprang forth. When I woke up, I realized a door had been opened unto me.

Whatever the problem was gave way. I made use of the truth that I knew.

> *"If ye had known me, ye should have known my father also; and from henceforth ye know him, and have seen him"* (John 14:7).

Quick access to what I needed was made available to me. God knows His own. My sheep hear my voice, and I know them and they follow me. His ears are always open to those who walk with Him and in the truth. You can't be in today with Him and be out tomorrow into the world. It's not done that way. Your legs have to be nailed with the truth. You must abide in Him, so He can abide in you. If you don't abide;

you can't be sanctified. *"Sanctify them in the truth; your word is truth"* (John 17:17). Our sanctification comes from Jesus Christ. The truth must sanctify you before you can have access to the Holy of the Holies. He alone brings purification to our spirits, soul, and body. He sets you apart for the work. But you have to be sponged by His Word (the truth).

> *"The sum of your word is truth, and every one of your righteousness rules endures forever"* (Ps. 119:160).

One of God's essential characteristics is truthfulness. He embodies perfect truth; therefore, His Word cannot lie. It is true and dependable for guidance and help. The Bible is the total compendium of who Christ Jesus is (the truth). In Him, there is no variability. His truth is food to our spirit when it is rightfully found. *"Thy truth was found, and I did eat them, and thy truth was unto me the joy and rejoicing of mine heart"* (Jer. 15:16).

Discovering the truth doesn't just bring us into the light, but it must be devoured. Let it take over your being. Let it synchronize every part of your cells. Until you have done so, then will you become delightful, both in your life and the people you come across. Allow the truth to pour Himself on you and internalize Himself. If we love and treasure God's Word, we should meditate on it diligently to know the truth.

> *"Stand therefore, having your loins girt about with truth, and having on the breastplate of righteousness"* (Eph. 6:14).

Be joyful when coming to have access to the truth. The disposition of your heart determines how you will make contact with the truth. His innermost thoughts can't be opened unto you if you're coming to Him is always about asking. He is not your cash-out. Be wise in your dealings. Be not cunning when you're in His presence or come with a deceitful heart.

> *"The Lord detests lying lips, but he delights in people who are trustworthy"* (Prov. 12:22).

The abundance of the truth you know makes you a foothold in God's Kingdom.

Section C

REST

Chapter 6

Perfection

"Be ye perfect, even as your father which is in heaven is perfect" (Matt. 5:48).

Your perfection is a resulting force of the truth abiding in you. You can't be perfect without Him; therefore, oneness must take place between you and the Holy One. The word *perfection* is made up of three parts:

Per–means "measure"

Fect–means "to do"

Ion–means "all"

When put together, *perfection* means "measure to do all." You must measure to do all. You must measure to be like Him. Remember that He created you in His image and likeness. The power to become is in you. You can't look elsewhere to be perfect. You can't meet the government to be perfect. You can't meet the scientist to be perfect. Most governments have not yet perfected their country or the people they rule. Every time they make promises that they can't keep, they keep giving these promises to their listeners. God has opened the door of perfection within you. You have to realize who you are in Christ Jesus. Isaac perceived who he was and he sowed in that land. He reaped a hundred folds of harvest because God was with him (Gen. 27:13). If the world rejects you, build yourself into a capacity to take them in. They will begin to look for you.

He became greater than the nation. Even then, he was later driven out because of jealousy. His people later looked for him as he was needed. The rejected stone became the chief corner stone. What he had within him and outside was not what they could neglect. I speak into your life that from today, your life will rise into all around perfection. Those who looked down at you will come begging you to rule over them in Jesus's name.

Jephthah was a man of valor (Judg. 11:1) in the presence of his people and unto God. He had no rest, which comes from being perfect in God. God was not his true existence. He believed so much in his strength and ability. A day came that a resultant force of not knowing God reflected in his life. His brethren who he grew up with rejected him.

> *"...And they thrust out Jephthah, and said unto him, thou shalt not inherit in our father's house for thou art the son of a strange woman"* (Judg. 11:2b).

The son of a strange woman became his description. That was not his fault; he didn't come to the world by himself. There must be a consummation between a man and a woman, but the driving force to that was *jealousy*. His brethren became jealous of him because he was a mighty man of valor.

He lacked perfection because he lacked God that created and controls institutions.

In Judges 11:3, Jephthah fled and dwelt in the land of Tob. He became a fugitive in a different land and experienced the beauty of rest. He encountered God through personalized dealing where he realized that God preserved him and questioned why he was running as he could have been killed. Tob in Hebrew means *mine*. He encountered God who made him His own; my rest, my perfection. He came to his senses that it was the mercy of God upon his life all along the journey.

> *"So, then it is not of him that willeth, nor of him that runneth, but of God that showeth mercy"* (Rom. 9:16).

A personalized dealing with God Almighty brought about a perfect rest in his life. If you read your Bible, you will see how God re-instituted him back to his father's house; not just that, he became judge of Israel (Judg. 11:5-12:7) for six years.

Most times, there are circumstances beyond your control that will force you away from the people you cherish so much and into life as an outcast. In this present dispensation, both believers and nonbelievers may drive away those who do not fit the norms dictated by society, neighborhoods, or churches. We often have lost Jephthahs in our communities due to jealousy or the prejudice of life that surrounds their birthing or background. Sometimes, most of them don't realize who they are, as a believer you need to help them find their place or rest in God, for their potential to be actualized. The reverse has become the order of the day. We say he is not my family or friend, in so doing, we have lost potable hands or lives to the kingdom of darkness. As a Christian, you know that everyone can have a place in God's family. What can you do to help people gain acceptance for their character and abilities?

> *"Love worketh no ill to his neighbor: therefore, love is the fulfilling of the law"* (Rom. 13:10).

Let's go back to the word *perfection*. I will give you a distinctive explanation as the Holy Spirit gives me revelational insight.

Per Means *"Measure"*

For a total rest in God as a believer, there is a weight of glory we need to have in Christ Jesus.

> *"For our light affliction, which is but for a moment, worketh for us a far more exceeding and eternal weight of glory"* (2 Cor. 4:17).

The light affliction signifies our present troubles that are small and won't last very long. But through such troubles lies perfection that leads us to our rest. The next line is where so many are interested in the weight of glory. You can say measure of glory. There is a full measure of glory to those who stand firm till the end. This measure of glory is for those who have decided no matter what condition they find themselves in, Christ Jesus is the headway.

Most believers have to focus on their pain rather than on the ultimate good. Do you know that athletes concentrate on the finish line and ignore their discomfort? We too must focus on the reward for our faith and the joy that lasts forever. No matter what happens to you in this life, we have the full measure of rest in Christ Jesus.

We are measured in His glory through our suffering, not in our monetary offering.

Fect means **"To Do"**

Before you are measured into His glory, you must do the will of the Father. There must be an accreditation. The voice of God must announce your diligence both in heaven and on Earth.

> *"This is my beloved son in whom I am well pleased"* (Matt. 3:17).

> *"For I came down from heaven not to do my own will, but of Him who sent me"* (John 6:38).

Our Lord Jesus made an emphasized statement to remind us that He didn't come to Earth for His purpose. The Word is a direct notification to all believers for you to be measured in His glory, you have to do. It is not a plea but a rule to enjoy the full weight of His glory.

For Joseph's dream to come to pass, he had to do what was necessary for his destiny. What must one do? He has to abstain from anything that is not the will of God. There is no shortcut to glory. For any shortcut, there is a long-cut knife waiting to lacerate your destiny into pieces.

In this journey, you can't do it all alone. The Holy One (Holy Spirit) must be invited into your life. Many temptations, problems, and arrows of darkness await us on that journey.

My sincere advice to you is to press on, no matter the circumstances. Paul said, *"I press toward the mark for the prize of the high calling of God in Christ Jesus"* (Phil. 3:14).

Our doings for the Kingdom's sake remove every undoing of darkness in our lives.

I see you marching forward.

Ion Means *"All"*

When you give God your all, He makes you tall among men. Therefore, there is a call in every individual's life to adhere to the Kingdom's voice to receive His all.

> *"But seek ye first the kingdom of God, and his righteousness; and all these things shall be unto you"* (Matt. 6:33).

Seek ye first means to prioritize. Make it more important, give your all. When you wake, let it be in your mind. When you walk, when you speak, it should be what comes out of you.

Let me give you an example: If you wake up in the morning and the first thing you do is light up a cigarette, it becomes a morning routine. That means you have prioritized it more than anything else. This is because anything you think about or do when you first wake or what you think about or do before you sleep has become your all. For you to be perfect, you need to have all of Christ Jesus inside of you.

> *"Blessed be the God and father of our Lord Jesus Christ, who hath blessed us with all spiritual blessings in heavenly places in Christ"* (Eph. 1:3).

To be blessed by all spiritual blessings in heavenly places, you must be infused with your all in Christ. With Christ Jesus, there is no limitation. He gives His all to those who will give their all to Him.

I urge you to submit your all to Him, to enjoy His all, in which lies His perfection.

Chapter 7

Joy

You can't be restful when you are not joyful.

Joy is not a one-day peace. It is an everlasting peace of happiness; a radiating smile that can spark or transmit a turnaround and hope in the life of others. *"They looked unto him and were radiant"* (Ps. 24:5). You can't look unto Him and remain the same. A rest that is full of joy must accompany you on your journey in life. Sorrow may be persisting in your life, but I assure you that joy must come.

> *"For his anger endureth but a moment; in his favour is life: weeping may endure for a night, but joy cometh in the morning"* (Ps. 30:5).

There cometh joy full of rest. It doesn't come at night. Joy is light, not darkness. That's why the Bible said, *"...joy cometh in the morning"* (Ps. 30:5). Change is a constant in life. Pain will be there, I know; I have been there. Joy is a permanent stay. Joy is the main occupant of our lives. The Holy Spirit brings that fruit into our life. Joy is a fruit of the Spirit. It can grow into an overflowing fountain.

"Shout with joy to the LORD, all the earth!" (Ps. 100:1).

When the spirit of joy rests in you, there must be a shouting. The joy in you begins to speak. It becomes loud and visible to the eyes of men. It can't be hidden. A true joy from the Lord is ever shining.

Joy makes us more grateful unto Him. Gratitude is seen in our lives. If gratitude is lacking, the person has not yet encountered joy. A person that has this can never be diminished when problems come their way. David is an example of this. He said, *"When anxiety was great within me, your consolation brought me joy"* (Ps. 94:19). You can't have joy and still be experiencing inner pain or defeat.

> *"Though the fig tree does not bud and there are no grapes on the vines, though the olive crop fails and the fields produce no food, though there are no sheep in the pen and no cattle in the stalls, yet I will rejoice in the LORD, I will be joyful in God my Saviour"* (Hab. 3:17-18).

Devastation will come or it's present in your life already. Allow the joy of God to flow into your heart. The above Bible verses state how prophet Habakkuk narrated his joy in God even though the physical provisions of life were not visible anymore, it would not stop him from rejoicing in Him. Habakkuk's feelings were not dominated by the events around him but by the faith in God's ability to give him strength. When nothing makes sense and when your troubles seem to be too much to bear, remember, God gives strength through the joy of the Spirit that is within us. You need to be joyful in hope and patient in affliction. It is a mandate for us, the believers, to be joyful always in the Lord.

> *"Rejoice in the Lord always. I will say it again. Rejoice!"* (Phil. 4:4).

When the Word of God repeats something twice, we need to seriously adhere to it. For you to encounter victory in Christ, you must remain joyful. Don't allow anything whatsoever to take away your joy. Delete friends that bring bad news into your life or words of competition, stirring up your heart into regret or sadness. Surround yourself with those that speak the message of hope, words of strength, and life.

> *"A man hath joy by the answer of his mouth; and a word spoken in due season, how good is it!"* (Prov. 15:23).

Out of one's mouth, a person speaks abundance of his heart. You can know if a person is joyful or not from the words that come out of his mouth. Words are life. It becomes most effective when spoken from a joyful heart. It is like a fountain of living water upon anywhere it goes. Your container, which is your body, feels the impact of joy within your spirit. You can't always be sad and your body always look or appear refreshed. No, that's not possible.

Maybe you have been spoken upon to be a prophet or God has told you that you will be used by Him to do great things here on Earth. My brethren, if you are not joyful, just forget about it. God uses those who are always joyful in the Spirit to carry out His assignments. Joy brings completeness to our well-being of life.

> *"I have told you this so that my joy may be in you and that your joy may become complete"* (John 15:11).

God is a rewarder of those that diligently, in joy, seek Him. In your diligence in seeking God, there is splendor in the heart and complete reward. Let there be an implant of joy within you.

In the next few verses of the Bible, the word *joy* will be infused in a strategic place in the Scripture. Please kindly follow me with your heart wide open.

> *"But Joy with contentment is great gain"* (1 Tim. 6:6).

The word *godliness* is what ought to be in place of joy. But I decided to put the word *joy* for better illustration. The joy within you comes with contentment. I know a family that had nothing. Anytime you saw them, there was a kind of happiness that comes with a transforming soul. When they smile and you are around where they are, you must smile. That is the true joy that I am speaking of; joy with contentment. Joy is contagious. You don't care what people say about you, your mind is set ready upon the Lord with a cheerful heart. Proverbs 17: 22 says, *"A cheerful heart is good medicine, but a crushed spirit dries up the bones."*

Rest is not permitted to come to you when the door of joy is not opened unto it. Rest responds to joy, a home full of joy has rest abide in there. When the door of joy is opened at home, rest opens up windows of blessings from heaven into that home. Rest is peace and peace bring in abundance. Look at the life of King Solomon. The Bible recorded that God gave him rest all around. Why? He gave a thousand burnt offerings unto God through a joyful heart. One Kings 3:6 is a profound verse for my illustration. It was not his offering but the heart in which he gave unto the Lord. He was glad that God chose him and established his throne instead of his brethren or the enemies of his father. His joy in giving brought to him wisdom that surpasses all before and after him. Riches beyond his wildest dreams were added to him.

> *"I rejoice in following your statutes as one rejoices in great riches"* (Ps. 119:14).

Following the statutes of God with joy brings about great riches.

My advice for you is to be joyful as I Thessalonians 5:16 says, *"Rejoice always."* Plant a seed of joy in your heart and family. Keep wetting with the Word of God to become a tree. A well-rooted tree cannot be easily pulled down by challenges.

Joy is the specter that we need to throw into the mind of God.

If you come to Him in prayer, you have to be joyful. When studying His Word, you must be joyful for the spirit of truth to reveal to you what you're reading.

Chapter 8

The Life

"Then Jesus declared, 'I am the bread of life. Whoever comes to me will never go hungry, and whoever believes in me will never be thirsty'" (John 6:35).

Why did the Lord declare that, "I am the bread of life?" The word *bread* was used instead of other staple food. Why bread then? Because in my wide scope of study and research, I discovered that the human race has been on a bread diet for thirty thousand years. It provides energy in the form of carbohydrates and other essential nutrients. I realized that people around the world eat bread to satisfy physical hunger and to sustain physical life. In that particular verse, Jesus Christ is telling us that, for His life to dwell in us, we have to welcome it into our lives with joy. In this way, we feel joyful when we see physical bread. We need to eat it, the way we eat physical bread. We have to digest the Word of God (the life), the way we digest the physical bread.

> *"Thy words were found, and I did eat them and thy word was unto me the joy and rejoicing of mine heart: For I am called thy name, O Lord God of hosts"* (Jer. 15:16).

Here, there must be adequate eating of the Word. The Word of God is the life of Christ we need. It transmits into the fullness of His life in us when we consistently eat the Word of God. We can satisfy spiritual hunger and sustain spiritual life only with a right relationship with Jesus Christ. No wonder He called Himself the Bread of Life. But bread must be eaten to sustain life, and Jesus must be invited into our daily lives to satisfy our hungry souls.

When you encounter the life of God in you, you must experience four things in your life which are:

- You must have the light of His life
- You must illuminate through His life

The Life

- *You must have the fullness of His life*
- *You must have the eternal life of Christ Jesus*

This is the acronym for **Life:**

L Stands for **Light**

I Stands for **Illumination**

F Stands for **Fullness**

E Stands for **Eternal**

When the **Light** comes inside of us, we **Illuminate** into His **Fullness** of His **Eternal** life.

His life was an exchange, not a change, giving us His life for our dying lives. He gave us a superior gift, which is why the word *change* is not used to describe what He did for us.

Change is to modify or alter a thing while the exchange is an act of giving one thing and receiving another, especially of the same type or value in return. Exchange is a classic example of Christ's death upon the cross. His life is more valuable for our sustainability and existence here on Earth. He took our miserable lives and gave us His precious life. His life became an exchange for our dominance, not a thing that we'll keep fixing.

LIGHT

"In him was life; and the life was the light of men. And the Light shineth in darkness; and the darkness comprehended it not" (John 1:4-5).

"The life was the light of men." Did you read that? How amazing as we are partaking of this wonderful gift called life. You can't start experiencing rest when you haven't witnessed the light of Christ Jesus in you. Let me show you something in a verse of the same Scripture.

"That was the true light, which lighteth every man that cometh into the world" (John 1:9).

It shows that other lights imitate the true light. Lucifer is the one that imitates the true light. Remember the Bible calls him the angel of light.

The Life

"And no marvel, for Satan himself is transformed into an angel of light" (2 Cor. 11:14).

When the angel of light (Satan) comes into a home, community, state, or nation, they begin to experience darkness without realizing it. Look at the land of Zebulon, the land of Naphtali, and Jordan of Galilee. The people thought they were in light, living their lives that way for centuries, without knowing that darkness had ruled over them. When the true light walked past, they saw a great light. The true light that gives great light is Jesus. The Bible recorded in Genesis 1:16 that God created two great lights: the greater governs the day and the lesser one at night. Jesus Christ is that greater light that beautifies our life as the morning. There is something about the morning. It brings hope that something unique will happen and also seeing another day the Lord has made.

The true light just walked, He didn't pray or speak a word. Have you allowed the true light to walk on the corridor of your life? If you allow Him to come in, your part will shine brighter and brighter unto a perfect day. He never passes without leaving His footprint that is full of light.

The readiness of your spirit to the light has qualified you to become a light to your world.

ILLUMINATION

"Now I have heard about you that a spirit of the gods is in you, and that illumination, insight and extraordinary wisdom have been found in you" (Dan. 5:14).

This verse of the Bible informs us how Daniel worked in the magnificence of the wisdom of God. The king said to Daniel, "that the spirit of gods is in you." For you to have rest, you must first welcome light into you, for you to illuminate. Daniel was illuminating the light of God in the land of Babylon. He so much allowed the true light to have a passage in his life and whenever the true light passed, he had to surely drop something or leave a footprint of His light. The man, Daniel, reigned in God's wisdom in a foreign land that alone distinguished him from others. He became a light that drove out the darkness in the land, Babylon. "And the light shineth in darkness" (John 1:5). Your illumination of the light of

God must cover any darkness. If you meet people and they do not have a change or don't encounter the light of God through you, you don't bear that light that illuminates or gives a gainful, lasting impact upon lives. You need to ask yourself; what is my spirit bearing? His Spirit must bear witness with our spirit, that we are sons of God. Are you?

FULLNESS

> *"And to know the love of Christ, which passeth knowledge, that ye might be filled with all fullness of GOD"* (Eph. 3:19).

Paul states that God's love is total; it reaches every corner of our experience. God's love is wide; it covers the breadth of our own experience and it reaches out to the whole world. God's love is everlasting; it extends throughout our lives and into eternity. God's love is high; it rises to the height of our celebration and elation. God's love is deep; it reaches the depths of our discouragement, despair, and even death. When you feel shut out or isolated, remember that you can never be lost in God's love. Our first experience of His fullness is His fullness.

He has loved us before the foundation of the earth was created. That means that God is love. He is the capsulated word called love. He exists in the inner and outer spheres of love.

You can't express love if you don't operate in the dynamics of God's love.

God's love finds complete expression only in Christ. In union with Christ and through His empowering spirit, we are complete. In Christ, we lack nothing, have nothing to lose, and have nothing to fear. We hail of the fullness of God available to us. But we must claim that fullness by living in touch with the Holy Spirit through faith and prayer each day.

The capacity of our Lord Jesus Christ's fullness brings about having the spiritual gifts that are already bestowed upon us through our Lord Jesus after His resurrection. We are God's masterpiece. He has created us and in Christ Jesus, so we can do the good things He planned for us long ago.

ETERNAL

> "These things I have written to you who believe in the name of the son of God. So that you may know that you have eternal life" (1 John 5:13).

God's promise gives us the certainty that we have eternal life through His Son. This truth doesn't depend on whether we feel close or far away from God. Eternal life comes from facts, not feelings. We can know that we have eternal life if we believe in God's truth. If you aren't sure that you are a Christian, ask yourself this:

Have I honestly committed my life to Him as my Savior and Lord? Does that decision affect your daily choices? If so, you know by faith that you are indeed a child of God.

Without eternal life in view, you can't have rest in due.

You must have the view (belief system) of eternity. Working with dignity for the Kingdom of God brings you into the fullness of eternity. Jesus Christ is life eternal.

There is a song we sing from my childhood that is so powerful to the soul. It goes like this:

"Eternal, Eternal Life (2x)
I want to live Eternal life,
God Save my soul,
I want to live Eternal life,
God save my soul."
Anonymous

I intentionally became a victim of God's seed to be saved. I can germinate into the life of eternity. Most of us don't have rest because our mindset is always to make money and have earthly possessions. All of these are vital. It is needed and I am not saying it's a sin. But it shouldn't be the cardinal point or view of existence. Matthew 6:33 says, *"But seek ye first the kingdom of God, and His righteousness and all these things shall be added unto you."*

He is always ready to give us the rest that we deserve. But are you ready to seek Him first? Surrender all that you have for the heavenly Kingdom's purpose. For instance, if you wanted to travel to a country for a short vacation using the USA as a case study. You must first have a valid visa to enter the country. When you get to the country's airport, there is a check point needed for you to pass through, that's the immigration rule of the country. If you obey and adhere to the rules of the country, your period of visitation will be restful because you obeyed the regulations of the country. You don't care if fifty police officers pass in front of you daily because, within you, you know all is well with the documents you have. That brings rest. How about the opposite? You can reflect on and answer this. Our focus point should be eternal life; things that are higher and better than earthly pleasure and temporal. Before I drop my pen, I will encourage you with this Bible Scripture; kindly read it with eternity in view and see eternal dwelling in your life.

> *"For our light affliction, which is but for a moment, worketh for us a far more exceeding and external weight of glory: While we look not at the things which are seen, but at the things which are not seen; for the things which are seen are temporal, but the things which are not seen are eternal"* (2 Cor. 4:17-18).

My kind advice to you is that you love that which surpasses above anything. Keep burning your sweet incense, and do not depart from it. Do this for the church and people around you through prayer for the evil days that will come their way.

J.C. Ryle said, *"Prayer should always interest Christians. It is the very life-breath of true Christianity."*

"The eternal Life of Christ is the essence of our salvation that He exists in us."

- Amanambu Kenechukwu

www.ingramcontent.com/pod-product-compliance
Ingram Content Group UK Ltd.
Pitfield, Milton Keynes, MK11 3LW, UK
UKHW042000230426
12048UKWH00009B/458